A CBO STUDY

Deforestation and Greenhouse Gases

January 2012

The Congress of the United States o Congressional Budget Office

Notes

All dollar values in this report are 2010 dollars.

Numbers in the text and figures may not add up to totals because of rounding.

The map shown on the cover of this report is from Adrian Deveny, Janet Nackoney, Nigel Purvis, and others, *Forest Carbon Index: The Geography of Forests in Climate Solutions* (Resources for the Future and Climate Advisers, December 2009).

Preface

Emissions of carbon dioxide, a greenhouse gas, come primarily from the consumption of fossil fuels and from deforestation. The destruction and degradation of forestland, caused mainly by expanded agricultural activity in tropical developing countries, currently accounts for an estimated 12 percent of global greenhouse gas emissions.

This Congressional Budget Office (CBO) study, prepared at the request of the Chairman of the Senate Committee on Foreign Relations, examines challenges that affect whether actions to preserve forests could make a cost-effective contribution to reducing global emissions of greenhouse gases. It also discusses the pros and cons of approaches that the United States and other developed countries could take to promote forest preservation. In keeping with CBO's mandate to provide objective, impartial analysis, the study contains no recommendations.

The report was written by Natalie Tawil of CBO's Microeconomic Studies Division, under the guidance of Joseph Kile and David Moore (formerly of CBO). Terry Dinan, Daniel Frisk, Ron Gecan, Ryan Miller, Bob Shackleton, and Chad Shirley, all of CBO, offered helpful comments, as did Molly Macauley of Resources for the Future and Brian Murray of Duke University. (The assistance of external reviewers implies no responsibility for the final product, which rests solely with CBO.)

Sherry Snyder edited the edited the report, and John Skeen proofread it. Maureen Costantino designed the cover and, with the assistance of Jeanine Rees, prepared the report for publication. Monte Ruffin printed the initial copies, and Linda Schimmel handled the print distribution. An electronic version is available on CBO's Web site (www.cbo.gov).

Douglas W. Elmendorf
Director

January 2012

Contents

Figures

Boxes

Summary

Human activities produce large amounts of greenhouse gases (GHGs), primarily carbon dioxide (CO_2), and thus contribute to global warming. The use of fossil fuels is the primary source of CO_2 emissions, but the removal of trees from forested land has also contributed.

Mature forests, having absorbed CO_2 from the atmosphere while growing, store carbon in wood, leaves, and soil. That carbon is released when people clear forested land and destroy the wood. From 2000 to 2005, the loss of forests, primarily in tropical developing countries, accounted for approximately 12 percent of global GHG emissions.

Slowing or halting deforestation in developing countries is a potentially low-cost way to help reduce global GHG emissions. For that potential to be realized, however, substantial challenges would need to be addressed—by providing technical and financial assistance to governments, by creating demand from private markets, or both.

Challenges in Reducing Forest-Based Emissions

If actions to support forest preservation are to play a cost-effective role in a significant international effort to reduce global GHG emissions, three broad challenges would have to be met:

■ Obtaining useful measurements of changes in the amount of carbon stored in forests,

■ Structuring incentives to reduce total forest-based emissions, and

■ Improving governance in developing countries.

Measuring Changes in Carbon Storage

Establishing programs to reduce emissions of greenhouse gases and assessing the effectiveness of those programs require methods for measuring emissions. In some cases, measuring them is easy—the electric power industry, for example, can use systems that directly, continuously, and accurately monitor CO_2 emissions.

Measuring emissions resulting from deforestation is more complicated, however, because such emissions depend on the amount of deforestation and the carbon content of the wood that has been destroyed. Researchers can combine remote-sensing data about the amount of deforestation with information about the carbon content of the wood gleaned from on-the-ground inventories of the number and size of trees in sample areas to make such measurements. Most developing countries would need to improve their technical capabilities to process remote-sensing data and conduct inventories in order to effectively implement any program aimed at reducing carbon emissions from deforestation.

Structuring Incentives to Reduce Total Forest-Based Emissions

To reduce total forest-based emissions worldwide, the design of preservation programs must consider not only how much additional preservation would result but also how much "leakage" would occur—that is, how much of a forest program's direct reductions in GHG emissions would be negated by additional GHG releases elsewhere.[1] For example, a program that compensates people for preservation in one location might prompt a decline in

---

1. Concerns about leakage are not unique to forest preservation programs. Leakage can also occur, for example, if sources subject to emission limits under national programs to lower greenhouse gas emissions relocate abroad to escape those limits, or if they lose market share to international competitors not subject to the limits.

Summary Figure 1.

Government Effectiveness in Countries Responsible for 95 Percent of Global Forest-Based Emissions, 1990 to 2005

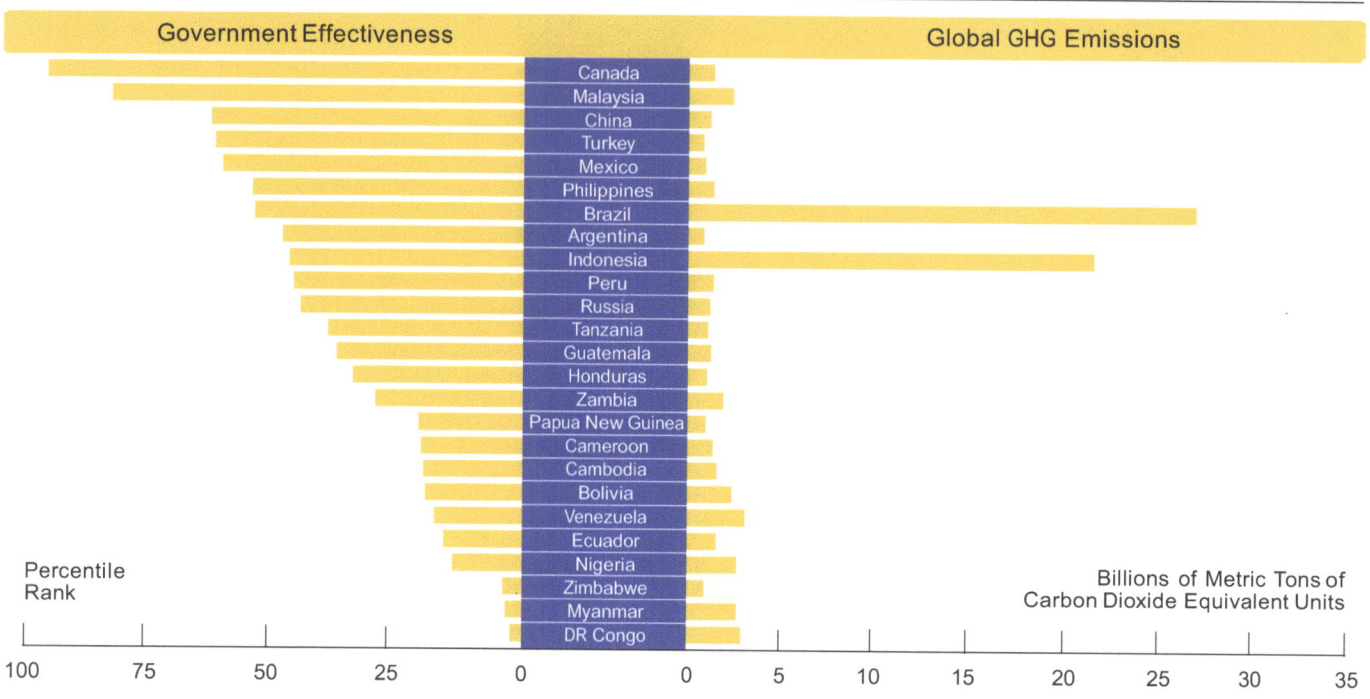

Sources: Congressional Budget Office based on data from World Bank, "Worldwide Governance Indicators" (2009), http://info .worldbank.org/governance/wgi/sc_country.asp; and World Resources Institute, "Climate Analysis Indicators Tool (CAIT)" (2011), http://cait.wri.org.

Notes: "Government effectiveness" is a governance indicator reported by the World Bank. It measures the quality of public services, the quality of the civil service and the degree of its independence from political pressures, the quality of policy formulation and implementation, and the credibility of the government's commitments to such policies.

GHG = greenhouse gas; DR Congo = Democratic Republic of the Congo.

the clearing of forested land for agriculture or timber production in that area, thus reducing supplies of those commodities and raising their prices. Higher prices, in turn, could encourage uncompensated landowners elsewhere to clear forests to produce agricultural products or timber to sell at the higher prices. Consequently, programs might need to compensate not only new preservation efforts aimed at threatened forests but also the continued preservation of forests that would not be threatened in the program's absence. Leakage reduces a program's cost-effectiveness, and significant leakage might negate the cost advantages that using forest preservation has in comparison with other approaches to achieving GHG reductions.

Improving Governance in Developing Countries

Weak governance—the inability to successfully design and implement policies to achieve stated objectives— undermines any efforts to use forest preservation programs to produce verifiable reductions in greenhouse gases. Even if they are motivated to participate in such programs, agencies in some developing countries may have inadequate authority for that task and may lack effective mechanisms for negotiating and distributing compensation to those who preserve forests. Also, the rights to any potential benefits from preserving forest resources may be poorly defined, making the gains from deforestation for agricultural and timber production and the use of wood for fuel more certain than the gains from preserving forests. Finally, government corruption and political instability can undermine laws that promote preservation.

Improving governance may be the most intractable of the three challenges. Of the 25 countries with the largest forest-based emissions in recent years, which together produced 95 percent of such emissions globally, nearly three-quarters rank in the bottom half of all countries on a key indicator of a country's ability to govern—government effectiveness. That indicator measures, for example, the quality of policy formulation and implementation and the credibility of the government's commitments to its policies. The World Bank, which tracks and reports measures of governance, rates the two largest emitters of forest-based CO_2—Brazil and Indonesia—at roughly the 50th percentile in terms of government effectiveness (see Summary Figure 1).

Policy Approaches for Reducing Forest-Based Emissions

Approaches the United States and other developed countries could take to encourage forest preservation in developing countries fall into two broad categories:

- Providing financial and technical assistance to governments interested in preserving forests and

- Creating demand in private markets for reductions in forest-based greenhouse gas emissions.

The two types of policies might work best together. The viability of markets, for example, may depend on having in place a reliable program for achieving measurable reductions in forest-based emissions—the type of program that financial and technical assistance can help establish.

Assistance to Governments

Financial and technical assistance can help overcome some of the challenges of pursuing forest preservation. It can help support advances in measuring and monitoring changes in forest carbon, help ensure that developing countries have access to the technologies for doing so, and also help counter leakage by offering incentives for achieving global reductions in forest-based emissions. Given uncertain funding and the challenges of improving governance in developing countries, the United States and other developed countries could consider focusing efforts on selected countries—for example, Brazil and Indonesia—that have relatively reliable governance, that are rich in remaining forest resources, and whose experiences could inform subsequent policy development.

Markets for Forest-Based Emissions

The United States and other developed countries could also generate resources for reducing forest-based GHG emissions by creating demand in private markets for such reductions. They could do that by establishing cap-and-trade programs or by taxing GHG emissions and providing tax credits for those who fund forest preservation activities. The potential for forest preservation in developing countries to lower the private-sector costs of achieving a goal for global GHG reductions might motivate substantial funding from private sources.

Deforestation and Greenhouse Gases

Emissions of greenhouse gases (GHGs) caused by human activity contribute to climate change. In particular, experts attribute most of the warming of the climate to emissions of carbon dioxide (CO_2). Although the use of fossil fuels for energy is the primary source of CO_2 emissions, the loss of forests is also a major contributor.

Forests affect the amount of CO_2 in the atmosphere in a number of ways.[1] As forests grow, they remove CO_2 from the atmosphere and absorb carbon into wood, leaves, and soil, where it can be stored for an extended period. When forests are cleared, stored carbon may be released into the atmosphere, depending in part on how much of the wood is destroyed. For example, using fires to clear forested land for agricultural production or other uses produces more emissions than does felling timber for wood products, which if disposed of in landfills at the end of their use will continue to store carbon.

The vast amount of carbon stored in forests worldwide indicates the important role of forests in climate change. The trees in forests are estimated to store the equivalent of roughly 760 billion metric tons of CO_2 worldwide—over one hundred times the United States' emissions of CO_2 and other greenhouse gases in 2009.[2] Most of the locations that are rich in forest carbon are in tropical countries (see the dark green areas in Figure 1). Preserving forests—by slowing or eliminating the loss of forests and the selective removal of trees (a process referred to as degradation)—would reduce CO_2 emissions.

Carbon storage in forests also can be increased by growing trees on previously unforested land (the brown areas shown in Figure 1). Globally, however, planting trees would contribute less to reducing concentrations of greenhouse gases in the atmosphere than would forest preservation. The potential for new forests to store carbon is limited by biological factors (such as the soil and climate conditions on available land) and economic factors (such as the benefits associated with current uses of that land that would have to be forgone if forests were planted).

For the same reasons, other forest-based activities—such as restoring degraded forests and practicing sustainable forest management—have even less potential to reduce concentrations of greenhouse gases in the atmosphere. Restoring degraded forests involves techniques that stimulate the natural regeneration of trees by reducing the intensity of grazing or planting selected areas with mixed tree species to help promote growth. Sustainable forest management, implemented on lands dedicated to timber production, involves practices such as reduced-impact logging, which includes limiting the slope of roads to prevent erosion, careful planning to minimize road building, and allowing trees to grow larger before harvesting them.

---

1. Forests also influence climate by providing a cooling effect through evaporation and a warming effect because their relatively dark surfaces reflect less solar radiation from the Earth's surface.

2. Adrian Deveny, Janet Nackoney, Nigel Purvis, and others, *Forest Carbon Index: The Geography of Forests in Climate Solutions* (Washington, D.C.: Resources for the Future and Climate Advisers, December 2009), Table A.6, p. 68, www.forestcarbonindex.org/RFF-Rpt-FCI_small.pdf. The estimate does not include carbon stored below ground in tree roots and in soil. Soil alone accounts for 49 percent to 84 percent of all carbon stored in forests—varying with latitude, forest type, and soil type—but not all carbon in soil is emitted when forests are destroyed. Carbon from soil can account for 10 percent or more of CO_2 emissions from deforestation and degradation; soil-based emissions are particularly important in northern forests and peat swamps. See Matthew Fagan and Ruth DeFries, *Measurement and Monitoring of the World's Forests: A Review and Summary of Technical Capability, 2009–2015* (Washington, D.C.: Resources for the Future, December 2009), www.rff.org/Publications/Pages/PublicationDetails.aspx?PublicatioID=20971; and Environmental Protection Agency, *Inventory of U.S. Greenhouse Gas Emissions and Sinks: 1990–2009*, USEPA 430-R-11-005 (April 2011), http://epa.gov/climatechange/emissions/usinventoryreport.html.

Figure 1.

Estimated Distribution of Carbon Storage in Forests

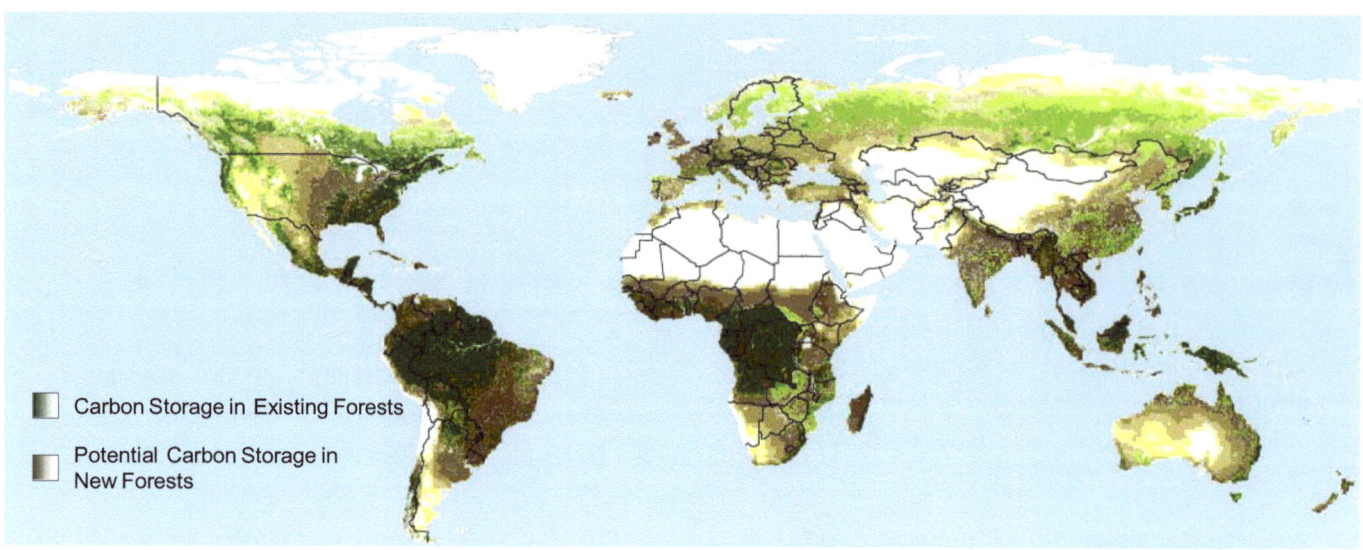

Carbon Storage in Existing Forests

Potential Carbon Storage in
New Forests

Source: Congressional Budget Office adapted from Adrian Deveny, Janet Nackoney, Nigel Purvis, and others, *Forest Carbon Index: The Geography of Forests in Climate Solutions* (Washington, D.C.: Resources for the Future and Climate Advisers, December 2009).

Note: The amount of carbon storage is greater in the dark green areas than in the lighter green areas; the potential for carbon storage is greater in the dark brown areas than in the lighter brown areas. Although forest growth is biologically possible in the brown shaded areas, planting trees there would not be a cost-effective way to store carbon on much of the land, given the land's limited potential to support forests and its value for other economic activities.

This Congressional Budget Office study examines the role of forest preservation in reducing global GHG emissions. It explores the challenges involved in establishing cost-effective programs to achieve such reductions and discusses policy approaches that the United States and other developed countries could take to encourage that effort.

Implications of Deforestation for Climate Change

Human activities lead to emissions of four principal greenhouse gases: carbon dioxide, methane, nitrous oxide, and a group of gases called halocarbons. Concentrations of those gases, which accumulate in the atmosphere, have increased in the industrial era. Carbon dioxide, the most prevalent of the four, accounts for roughly three-quarters of the impact of greenhouse gases on climate, largely because it is a by-product of burning fossil fuels but also because it is released when forests are cleared and the wood is destroyed.

One widely cited estimate of the impact of net forest loss during the 1990s, for example, put its share of global

GHG emissions—measured in terms of the impact on warming—at 20 percent, within a likely range of 6 percent to 34 percent.[3] That estimate averaged two assessments—one based on ground-level forest inventories (the counting and measuring of trees in sample plots) undertaken by countries and reported to the United

---

3. K.L. Denman and others, "Couplings Between Changes in the Climate System and Biogeochemistry," in S. Solomon and others, eds., *Climate Change 2007: The Physical Science Basis* (contribution of Working Group I to the Fourth Assessment Report of the Intergovernmental Panel on Climate Change, Cambridge University Press, 2007), www.ipcc.ch/publications_and_data/ar4/wg1/en/ch7.html.

The impact of one ton of emissions of a greenhouse gas on climate differs depending on how that particular gas affects the balance within the Earth's atmosphere between incoming solar radiation and outgoing infrared radiation. To account for that difference, researchers report all GHG emissions in terms of carbon dioxide equivalent, or CO_2e. Because greenhouse gases vary in how long they stay in the atmosphere, that equivalence depends on the period over which the contribution of a metric ton is measured. By convention, CO_2e is usually measured over 100 years. A metric ton of CO_2e is the amount of a given greenhouse gas that makes the same contribution to global warming as a metric ton of CO_2.

Figure 2.

Estimated Shares of Global Emissions of Greenhouse Gases Caused by Human Activity, by Source, 2005

(Percent)

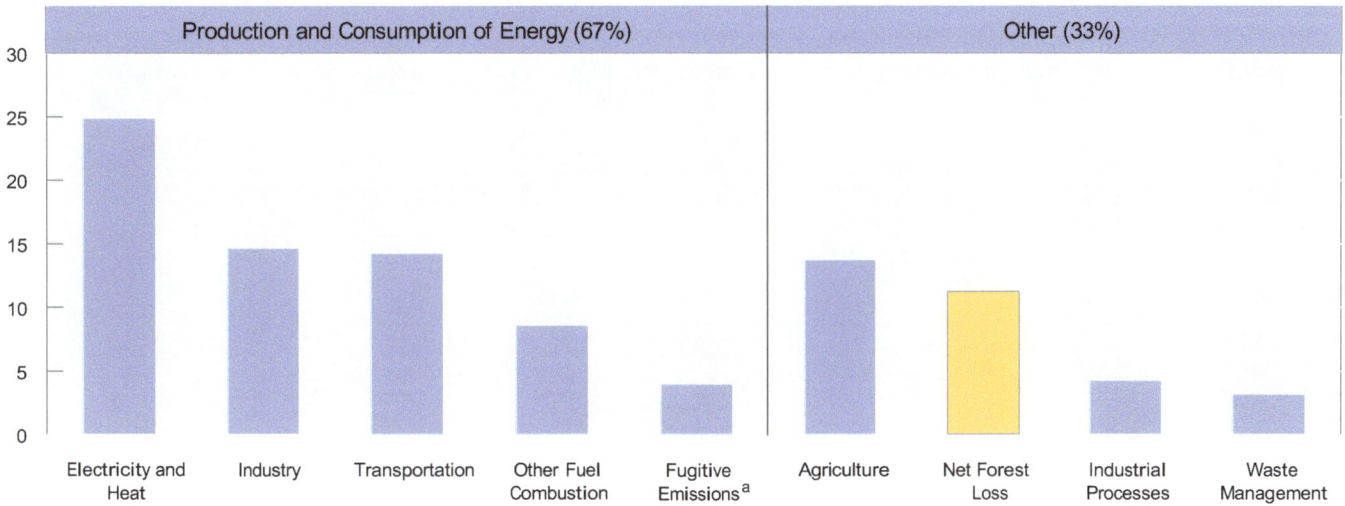

Source: Congressional Budget Office based on data from World Resources Institute, World Greenhouse Gas Emissions: 2005 (Washington, D.C.: WRI, December 2005), www.wri.org/chart/world-greenhouse-gas-emissions-2005.

Note: The impact on climate of one ton of emissions of a greenhouse gas depends on how that particular gas affects the balance within the Earth's atmosphere between incoming solar radiation and outgoing infrared radiation. To assess the impact of all greenhouse gases on an equal basis, researchers report emissions in terms of carbon dioxide equivalent, or CO_2e. This figure shows the share of emissions from various sources measured in terms of metric tons of CO_2e. A metric ton of CO_2e is the amount of a given greenhouse gas that has the same impact on climate as a metric ton of CO_2. (A metric ton equals 1.1 tons.)

a.   Fugitive emissions are those associated with the production, processing, storage, transmission, and distribution of fossil fuels such as oil, natural gas, and coal (including abandoned underground coal mines).

Nations' Food and Agriculture Organization (FAO) and the other based on data gathered by remote-sensing instruments. That 20 percent estimate was later revised downward—to 16 percent—reflecting corrected FAO data indicating that the amount of tropical deforestation during that period was less than originally thought.[4]

A subsequent assessment, for the 2000–2005 period, produced an even lower estimate of the impact of net forest loss, putting its share at 12 percent of global GHG emissions measured in terms of the impact on warming, within a likely range of 6 percent to 17 percent.[5] The estimate was lower than the estimate in the 1990s mainly because of higher emissions from the combustion of fossil fuels rather than a decline in deforestation.

That 12 percent estimate is similar to the warming impact of global GHG emissions from agriculture, including methane (from animal waste) and nitrous oxide (from the use of fertilizer). That estimate is also similar to estimates of effects from global energy use in industry and transportation (see Figure 2).

Estimates of the contribution of forest loss to global GHG emissions are more uncertain than are estimates for many other sources. Electric utilities, for example, can use systems that directly, continuously, and accurately monitor CO_2 emissions. By contrast, estimates of forest-based emissions are made indirectly because there is no way to measure the emissions from forest loss. Instead, researchers measure forest loss itself and use that as a basis for estimating emissions. Moreover, measurements of forest loss are derived from samples rather than from evaluations of the entire forest, so they are subject to error. For example, one particular challenge in measuring forest-based emissions is effectively accounting for the degradation of

---

4.   G.R. van der Werf and others, "CO_2 Emissions from Forest Loss," *Nature Geoscience,* vol. 2 (November 2009), pp. 737–738.

5.   Ibid.

Figure 3.

Ranking of Countries by Their Estimated Contribution to Global Forest-Based Emissions, 1990 to 2005

(Percent)

Sources: Congressional Budget Office based on data from World Resources Institute, "Climate Analysis Indicators Tool (CAIT)" (2011), http://cait.wri.org. For details, see World Resources Institute, CAIT: GHG Sources and Methods (Washington, D.C.: WRI, November 2010), http://cait.wri.org/downloads/cait_ghgs.pdf; and World Bank, World Development Report: Development and Climate Change, Selected Indicators, Table A2 (Washington, D.C.: World Bank, 2010), http://siteresources.worldbank.org/INTWDR2010/Resources/5287678-1226014527953/WDR10-Full-Text.pdf.

Notes: Researchers use regional and global estimates of changes in land use to derive estimates for forest-based emissions of the 25 largest national contributors. They typically base the country estimates on a single data point for each year in the period, and errors associated with the estimates may be substantial.

Emissions of greenhouse gases are measured in terms of carbon dioxide equivalent (CO_2e). A metric ton of CO_2e is the amount of a given greenhouse gas that makes the same contribution to global warming as a metric ton of CO_2. (A metric ton equals 1.1 tons.)

PNG = Papua New Guinea.

Current Locations and Causes of Deforestation

forests. Selective removal of certain tree species from mature forests reduces carbon storage but is difficult to detect compared with the changes in land cover associated with more complete clearing of forested land.

About 95 percent of forest-based emissions come from 25 countries, most of which are developing countries in the tropics (see Figure 3). Researchers estimate that about three-quarters of all tropical deforestation stems from the clearing of land for agricultural production, ranging from large-scale businesses to subsistence farming.[6] In South America, for example, large agricultural businesses clear forests to raise beef cattle and to grow soybeans and other crops for domestic and international markets. In Southeast Asia, land is cleared for large-scale farming to produce palm oil and coffee for international markets and for smaller producers to grow crops for domestic markets. Southeast Asia is also an important supplier of timber to international markets.

6. S. Solomon and others, eds., *Climate Change 2007: The Physical Science Basis* (contribution of Working Group I to the Fourth Assessment Report of the Intergovernmental Panel on Climate Change, Cambridge University Press, 2007), www.ipcc.ch/publications_and_data/publications_ipcc_fourth_assessment_report_wg1_report_the_physical_science_basis.htm.

Figure 4.

Estimated CO₂ Emissions for the Top CO₂-Emitting Nations, 1990 to 2005

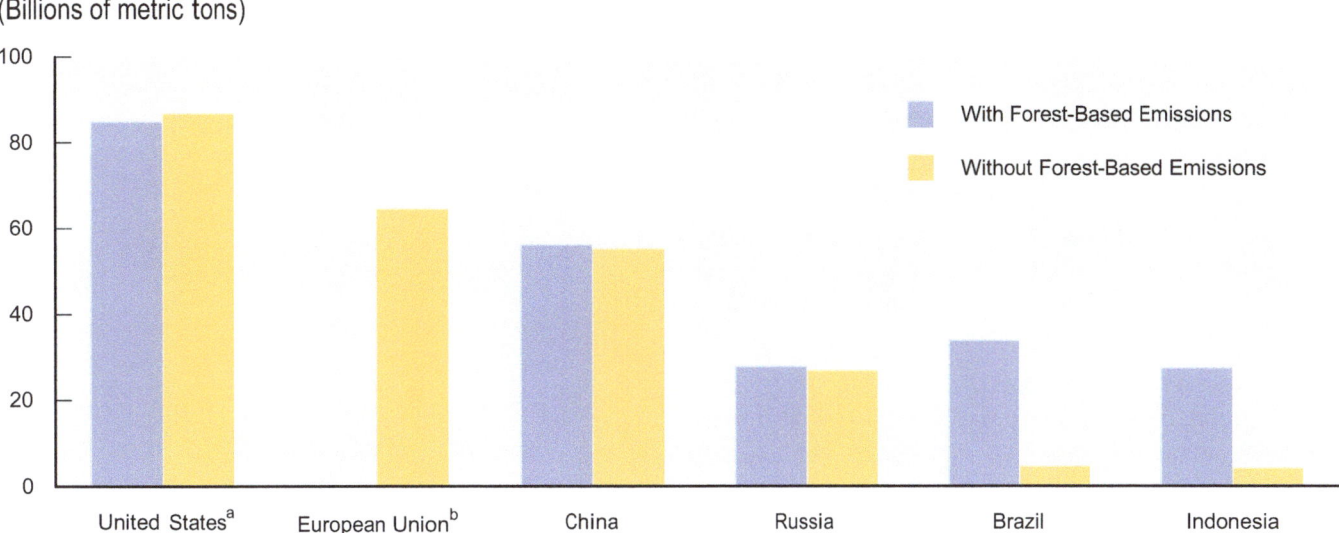

(Billions of metric tons)

Source: Congressional Budget Office based on data from World Resources Institute, "Climate Analysis Indicators Tool (CAIT)" (2011), http://cait.wri.org.

Notes: A metric ton equals 1.1 tons.

CO₂ = carbon dioxide.

a. In the United States, a net gain in forest area lowered total estimated CO₂ emissions over the 1990–2005 period.

b. Data on forest-based CO₂ emissions are not available for members of the European Union, but those countries experienced a net gain in forest area over the 1990–2005 period. Data on CO₂ emissions other than forest-based emissions are for the 27 countries that belonged to the European Union in 2005, even if they had not been members for the entire 1990–2005 period. Those countries are Austria, Belgium, Bulgaria, Cyprus, the Czech Republic, Denmark, Estonia, Finland, France, Germany, Greece, Hungary, Ireland, Italy, Latvia, Lithuania, Luxembourg, Malta, the Netherlands, Poland, Portugal, Romania, Slovakia, Slovenia, Spain, Sweden, and the United Kingdom.

By contrast, most farming in Africa is done on a smaller scale, and it is local communities rather than large businesses that typically encroach on forests as a source of farmland. About 70 percent of Africans depend on small-scale agriculture and the harvesting of natural resources for their livelihood.[7] In addition, 75 percent of urban households and over 90 percent of rural households in sub-Saharan Africa depend on wood, crop residues, and charcoal as their primary source of energy.[8]

In South America and Southeast Asia, deforestation in Brazil and Indonesia is the principal source of forest-based emissions. From 1990 to 2005, forest-based emissions from those two countries were significant enough to place them in the ranks of the top CO₂-emitting nations in the world—along with the United States, China, Russia, and the nations of the European Union combined (see Figure 4). In contrast, on the basis of CO₂ emissions related to fossil fuel alone, Brazil and Indonesia ranked 19th and 21st, respectively.[9]

The economic motivation to clear forests is evident. For individual farmers or landowners, increasing agricultural production by clearing forested land yields tangible benefits in the near term by providing food for consumption and products for sale in local, domestic, and international markets. From a national perspective, agriculture accounts for a large share of gross domestic product (GDP) in tropical developing countries. From 1990 to

7. Hilda Munyua, *ICTs and Small-Scale Agriculture in Africa: A Scoping Study* (prepared for the International Development Research Centre, 2008), http://web.idrc.ca/uploads/user-S/12212542261Final_Report_HMunya.pdf.

8. R. Bailis and others, "Mortality and Greenhouse Gas Impacts of Biomass and Petroleum Energy Futures in Africa," *Science,* vol. 308 (April 1, 2005), pp. 98–103.

9. World Resources Institute, "Climate Analysis Indicators Tool (CAIT)" (2011), http://cait.wri.org.

2005, agriculture's annual average share of GDP was 7 percent (about $47 billion) in Brazil and 17 percent (about $31 billion) in Indonesia.[10]

In some cases, government subsidies add to the market incentives that encourage agricultural production. Such subsidies reduce the private costs of growing certain kinds of crops, increasing the profits available from that production and thereby providing additional incentives to clear forests. In Indonesia, for example, government policies have supported production of biofuel feedstocks (the main raw materials used in producing biofuels), such as oil palm (the trees from whose fruits palm oil is extracted), by charging below-market interest rates to subsidize loans for developing plantations; by establishing mandatory shares of biofuel use in transportation, industry, and electric power generation; and by funding research and development. The land most suitable for planting oil palm is lowland evergreen tropical rainforest, and about 6 percent of land cleared in Indonesia from 1990 to 2005 was deforested for that purpose.[11] More generally, policies for reducing GHG emissions that promote the expansion of biofuel production but do not assign a value to forest preservation could have the unintended effect of increasing GHG emissions by encouraging deforestation so that land could be cleared for producing biofuel feedstocks (see Box 1).

In contrast, the market incentives for preserving forests are weak. Unlike the benefits of agricultural production, which accrue primarily to producers in the near term, the benefits of preserving forests accrue globally over the longer term by helping to counter climate change and minimize the damage associated with it. Unlike agriculture, efforts to preserve forests lack well-established mechanisms for compensating those who opt for preserving the forest rather than clearing the land. From 2007 to 2010, for example, market-based compensation for climate-related forest preservation averaged an estimated $28 million annually, which was generated through vol-

untary programs for reducing GHG emissions. That sum is equal to only 0.04 percent of the $78 billion that agriculture contributes annually to the combined GDP of Brazil and Indonesia.[12] And compared with agriculture's annual contribution of approximately $167 billion to the combined GDP of the 21 tropical developing countries experiencing deforestation, the $28 million in compensation is even less significant—just 0.02 percent.

Governments of developing countries and landowners in those countries incur costs when they choose to preserve forests. Governments, for example, incur the costs of establishing programs to monitor forests and enforcing laws that protect them. They may also be reluctant to increase forest preservation because of concerns about whether the distribution of associated benefits among individuals, groups, or regions might create political tensions. Landowners incur the costs of not using the land in other ways—giving up income from the sale of agricultural products, for example. But governments and landowners could also benefit from compensation offered for maintaining the carbon stored in forests and by contributing to efforts to reduce the damage caused by climate change. The balance of costs and benefits would be a significant determinant in their decisions about land use and about participating in an emission-reduction program related to deforestation.

Forests and Cost-Effective Reductions in Greenhouse Gases

Reducing forest-based emissions in developing countries is widely considered to be a relatively inexpensive way to reduce emissions of greenhouse gases even though esti- mates of the cost-effectiveness of that approach are very uncertain. Because climate change occurs on a global scale, the climate *benefits* of a reduction in GHG

10. World Bank, World dataBank, "World Development Indicators & Global Development Finance," http://databank.worldbank.org/ ddp/home.do?Step=12&id=4&CNO=2.

11. Lian Pin Koh and David S. Wilcove, "Is Oil Palm Agriculture Really Destroying Tropical Biodiversity?" *Conservation Letters*, vol. 1, no. 2 (June 2008), pp. 60–64, http://onlinelibrary .wiley.com/doi/10.1111/j.1755-263X.2008.00011.x/abstract.

12. See Katherine Hamilton, Molly Peters-Stanley, and Thomas Marcello, *Building Bridges: State of the Voluntary Carbon Markets* (Washington, D.C.: Ecosystem Marketplace, 2008, 2009, 2010), www.ecosystemmarketplace.com. For data for 2007 to 2009, see Alexandre Kossoy and Philippe Ambrosi, *State and Trends of the Carbon Market 2010* (World Bank: Washington, D.C., May 2010), http://siteresources.worldbank.org/ INTCARBONFINANCE/Resources/State_and_Trends_of _the_Carbon_Market_2010_low_res.pdf.

Box 1.

Biofuels and Greenhouse Gas Emissions

Proponents of policies that promote the use of biofuels argue that substituting those renewable energy sources for fossil fuels can help reduce greenhouse gas (GHG) emissions. Growing biofuel feedstocks—the raw materials, such as corn, sugarcane, switchgrass, oil palms, and soybeans, used to produce biofuel—draws carbon dioxide (CO_2) out of the atmosphere in amounts equal to the emissions produced when the biofuel is burned, whereas using fossil fuels produces net emissions of CO_2. If policies promote the expansion of biofuels but do not place a value on forest preservation, deforestation could spread—increasing associated GHG emissions—as land is cleared for producing the more profitable biofuel feedstocks.

Thus, a key factor in assessing the impact of biofuels on GHG emissions is accounting for the previous use of the land on which the feedstock is grown. If the land was converted from peat, grasses, or forest, that change in land use would boost GHG emissions. Some researchers maintain that it could take decades, or even centuries, before the emission reductions associated with the use of biofuels compensate for the increased emissions from changes in land use. Others conclude that the use of biofuels could result in net reductions in GHG emissions over shorter periods (see the table below).

Estimated Time Required for the Use of Biofuels to Lower Greenhouse Gases When Forestland Is Cleared to Grow Feedstocks

Land Cleared	Location	Years Until Net GHG Reduction[a]	Study
Sugarcane Ethanol			
Rainforest	Brazil	45	Searchinger and others
Forest	Brazil	44	Lapola and others
Forest	Brazil	15 to 39	Renewable Fuels Agency
Forest	Brazil	17	Fargione and others
Palm Biodiesel			
Forest	Brazil	86	Fargione and others
Forest	Malaysia	18 to 38	Renewable Fuels Agency
Soybean Diesel			
Forest	Brazil	319	Fargione and others
Forest	Brazil	246	Lapola and others

Source: Congressional Budget Office, Using Biofuel Tax Credits to Achieve Energy and Environmental Policy Goals (July 2010), using information from Timothy Searchinger and others, "Use of U.S. Croplands for Biofuels Increases Greenhouse Gases Through Emissions from Land-Use Change," Science, vol. 319 (2008), pp. 1238–1240; David M. Lapola and others, "Indirect Land-Use Changes Can Overcome Carbon Savings from Biofuels in Brazil," Proceedings of the National Academy of Sciences, vol. 107, no. 8 (February 8, 2010), pp. 3388–3393; Renewable Fuels Agency, The Gallagher Review of the Indirect Effects of Biofuels Production (study commissioned by the Secretary of State for Transport, United Kingdom, July 2008); and Joseph Fargione and others, "Land Clearing and the Carbon Debt," Science, vol. 319 (2008), pp. 1235–1238.

Note: GHG = greenhouse gas.

a.   The number of years a biofuel would have to be used before the cumulative GHG emissions associated with that biofuel would be lower than the cumulative GHG emissions associated with the use of fossil fuels instead.

emissions do not depend on either the location of the reduction or the type of source from which it is generated. The *cost* of that reduction, however, depends on both factors. If there were a significant international effort to counter climate change, identifying relatively inexpensive options for reducing global GHG emissions could help lower the total cost of that undertaking.[13]

The climate policies of other countries and their evolution over time would, however, be critically important to achieving an effective reduction in global emissions of greenhouse gases. Unless a significant percentage of the world's economy restricted emissions, the beneficial effects on climate of any forest-based reduction in emissions could be undermined by emissions from other sources. Although forest preservation can play an important role in many activities—maintaining biodiversity, for example—it is only one strategy among many that would have to be used in a comprehensive global effort to reduce GHG emissions and avert some of the potential damage to the environment and the attendant economic losses associated with climate change.

Cost-Effectiveness of Reducing Forest-Based Emissions

Analyses of cap-and-trade programs that the Congress has considered indicate that reducing forest-based GHG emissions may be a relatively inexpensive way to reduce overall emissions. In such programs, the government sets a cap, or limit, on the amount of GHG emissions that can be produced over a given period. It then distributes rights to emit the gases, or "allowances," by either selling the allowances or giving them away to businesses that must comply with the limits. Businesses can comply with the limits on GHG emissions by submitting one allowance for each ton of CO_2e they emit. Businesses that reduce their emissions at a cost below the price of allowances can sell their rights to emit greenhouse gases, and those with higher costs can buy allowances.

Businesses can also comply with the limits by using "offsets," which substitute alternative, less expensive reductions in emissions for those from the businesses that have to comply with the program. Those alternative reductions can be forest-based (for example, from preserving forests to minimize releases of CO_2),

agriculture-based (from reducing emissions of methane from animal waste), or industry-based (from controlling methane emissions from landfills). By changing the mix of activities undertaken to achieve the GHG limits, offsets increase the available supply of allowances, lower their price, and reduce the total cost of meeting the program's specified GHG limits.

The Environmental Protection Agency's (EPA's) estimates of allowance prices under draft cap-and-trade legislation illustrate the potential of offsets, including those from forest preservation, to lower the cost of reducing greenhouse gas emissions. In making its estimates, EPA assumed that actions to reduce such emissions would be widespread and would be taken by developed and developing countries. Allowing offsets from forest preservation would reduce the price of allowances (and the cost of complying with the proposed caps) by 20 percent, EPA estimated.[14] Without such offsets, businesses that had to comply would increase their own emission reductions and purchase more offsets from domestic sources—both of which are more expensive methods of compliance than is forest preservation in developing countries.

Uncertainty About the Cost-Effectiveness of Reducing Forest-Based Emissions

Estimates by EPA and others of the potential cost-effectiveness of a policy that promotes forest-based mitigation are uncertain because quantifying the potential of forests to store carbon involves many factors that are difficult to assess. Those factors include an estimate of what forest-based emissions would be in the absence of the policy, the value of the land in alternative uses over time, the direct costs of undertaking the conservation practices and verifying the results, policies in countries around the world, and the impact of climate change itself.

Determining potential emission reductions, for example, requires a baseline from which to measure those reductions; that is, an estimate of what forest-based emissions would be in the absence of the policy. Such baselines are uncertain because recent estimates of the contribution of

---

13. See Congressional Budget Office, *The Costs of Reducing Greenhouse Gas Emissions*, Issue Brief (November 2009).

14. Environmental Protection Agency, Office of Atmospheric Programs, *EPA Analysis of the American Power Act in the 111th Congress* (June 14, 2010; revised June 30, 2010), www.epa.gov/climatechange/economics/pdfs/EPA_APA_Analysis_6-14-10.pdf. In that accounting, the use of offsets from developing countries for compliance would decline by nearly 70 percent.

forest-based emissions to global GHG releases range from 6 percent to 17 percent. Lower (or higher) baseline emissions would imply lesser (or greater) potential for reducing emissions from deforestation.

The costs of preserving forests as a way to mitigate climate change are also difficult to assess. They depend on the value of the land in alternative uses—that is, the opportunity costs, the benefits forgone when forests are left standing rather than being cleared for agricultural production or the harvesting of timber for wood products or for fuel. Opportunity costs change over time depending on economic, social, and institutional conditions such as population, technology, income, trade, and government policies. The models researchers use to estimate costs ideally would account for those factors over time, but assumptions about the future may plausibly differ and may have varying influences on cost estimates.

Estimates of the costs of forest-based mitigation also depend on the direct costs of putting preservation practices in place, such as those incurred in patrolling protected forests, and the costs of verifying the results of such practices. Verification includes determining whether the forest-based reductions in emissions of greenhouse gases would have occurred even in the absence of the incentives offered by the program, the extent to which the reductions are neutralized by program-related increases in emissions of greenhouse gases in other locations, and whether they are reliably measured over time. Although no standard definition of the costs of verification is widely accepted and no consensus has emerged on how to quantify or predict them, many experts believe that they are not high enough to negate the cost-effectiveness of some amount of forest-based mitigation.[15]

The cost-effectiveness of forest-based mitigation for the United States also depends on how other countries choose to use forests to achieve whatever goals they might have for reducing GHG emissions. Those choices could influence the amount of forest preservation that developing countries decide to undertake and how much developed countries are willing to pay to support that preservation—both of which will affect the cost of forest-based reductions in greenhouse gas emissions.

Finally, a changing climate itself would probably have an impact on the cost-effectiveness of forest-based mitigation. The location of forests, their species composition, and their productivity in storing carbon could be affected by changes in temperature, precipitation, and other factors that affect the health of forests. How the various effects of GHG emissions will affect forests over centuries is very uncertain. Forests could expand in some areas and contract in others, depending on the net effect of those influences. For instance, the growth rate of trees could increase as the amount of carbon dioxide in the atmosphere increases, although rates may eventually plateau as trees adjust to the new levels. However, existing forests may be threatened by changes in precipitation patterns. Those changing patterns and higher temperatures could also increase the number of forest fires. Similarly, diseases and pests that attack trees could become a greater threat in a warming climate.

Challenges in Reducing Forest-Based Emissions

Policies aiming to reduce global emissions of greenhouse gases by encouraging forest preservation in developing countries could impose costs or offer compensation as an incentive to reduce emissions. But, having other countries impose costs on developing countries to promote forest preservation would be very controversial. Forests are resources that many countries—including developed countries—have used in pursuing economic development. In addition, many developed countries have per capita GHG emissions that are higher than those of the developing countries that have large stores of carbon in their forests, suggesting that it would be seen as unfair treatment of nations that were poorer and had lower GHG emissions. Policies providing compensation to motivate efforts to preserve forestland would not raise such concerns, and the remainder of this section focuses on challenges involved in implementing such policies.

Three challenges would make it difficult to reduce forest-based emissions cost-effectively:

■ Measuring changes in the amount of carbon stored in forests,

■ Structuring incentives to reduce total forest-based emissions, and

■ Improving governance in developing countries.

---

15. For more information about the costs of verification, see Congressional Budget Office, *The Use of Offsets to Reduce Greenhouse Gases,* Issue Brief (August 2009).

Measuring Changes in Carbon Storage

Forest-based mitigation programs need measurements of how the amount of carbon stored in forests in a country changes over time. Some experts conclude that advances in measurement techniques may reduce uncertainty enough within the next decade that such measurements would be useful for mitigation programs.[16]

Current Measurement Approaches. The amount of carbon stored in a forest depends on the product of four factors—the area, volume, and biomass of the forest, and the carbon content of the biomass:

Forest Carbon = Forest Area x Forest Volume x Forest Biomass x Carbon Content of Biomass.

Area is the amount of land covered by trees, and volume—the amount of wood—per unit of area depends on the size of the trees. The biomass—the living plant material produced from water and CO_2 by photosynthesis—per unit of volume depends on the density of the wood, which is influenced by factors such as a tree's location and species; carbon represents roughly half of that biomass.

Area and Volume of Forests. Data for estimating area and volume can come from on-the-ground inventories, in which trees in sample areas are counted and measured. The FAO compiles its Forest Resources Assessment every five years using forest inventories provided by individual countries. The quality of the country reports varies, however; not all countries identify forests using the FAO's definition.[17] Further, some countries may not have the resources needed to properly conduct inventories. Among the 50 nations with the greatest volume of wood in forests in 2005, 15 reported a loss in forest area between 1990 and 2005 but no accompanying change in volume per unit of area, suggesting that they may have simply assumed a constant volume over the 15-year period instead of reassessing that figure.[18]

Instruments mounted on airplanes or satellites also can provide data for estimating a forest's area and volume. Researchers can combine the data gathered by such remote-sensing activities with information from forest inventories to produce their estimates. Remote-sensing can cover a broader geographic scope and generate data more frequently than can an inventory. Standard remote-sensing technologies, which essentially offer a two-dimensional view of the forest from above, provide relatively good measures of forest area but not of forest volume. The U.S. Landsat program, started in 1972, is the longest continuously operating satellite system for observing the Earth. Landsat produces images using visible light and the heat radiated from objects on the Earth's surface. Using those data, researchers can estimate a forest's *area* with about 80 percent to 90 percent accuracy; in contrast, the accuracy of estimates of forest *volume* based on the data can be as low as 40 percent in forests with mixed species and overlapping tree canopies.[19] An important limitation of the data collected by Landsat is that the satellite's instruments cannot penetrate the clouds and smoke that often cover tropical rainforests.

More advanced and more expensive remote-sensing technologies can provide better measures of a forest's volume. Those instruments transmit pulses of radio waves (in the case of synthetic aperture radar, or SAR) or light from a laser (in the case of light detection and ranging, or LIDAR, technology) that can penetrate clouds, smoke, and the tree canopy to gather data on how objects on the Earth's surface reflect the emitted energy. SAR and LIDAR deliver a three-dimensional view of a forest and can be used to measure the elevation of the underlying land and the height of trees, allowing researchers to estimate the volume of forests with greater than 80 percent accuracy. Currently, only about nine SAR systems and one LIDAR system are operating on satellites, but that

16. Molly Macauley and others, *Forest Measurement and Monitoring: Technical Capacity and "How Good Is Good Enough"* (Washington, D.C.: Resources for the Future, December 2009), www.rff.org/rff/documents/rff-rpt-technical%20capacity_macauley%20et%20al.pdf.

17. FAO defines a forest as "land spanning more than 0.5 hectares with trees higher than 5 meters and a canopy cover of more than 10 percent, or trees able to reach these thresholds (in place)." See Food and Agriculture Organization of the United Nations, *Global Forest Resources Assessment 2010* (Rome: FAO, October 2010), www.fao.org/forestry/fra/fra2010/en.

18. P. Kauppi and others, "Returning Forests Analyzed with the Forest Identity," *Proceedings of the National Academy of Sciences*, vol. 103, no. 46 (November 14, 2006), pp. 17574–17579, http://phe.rockefeller.edu/docs/PNAS-Forests_final.pdf.

19. See Fagan and DeFries, *Measurement and Monitoring of the World's Forests.* For forest area, "accuracy" refers to the percentage of pixels in the imagery that correctly identify the type of land cover; for forest volume, "accuracy" refers to the match between predictions from remote imagery and actual ground measurements.

may change; among the current plans that countries around the world have for satellite missions between 2009 and 2016, 25 missions have SAR, two have LIDAR, and one has both.[20]

Biomass per Unit of Forest Volume. Data for estimating biomass per unit of volume come from statistical relationships that researchers have established by measuring, harvesting, drying, and weighing trees. The relationships used to estimate biomass in tropical forests—many of which contain 300 or more species of trees—are based on a limited sample of trees, and some researchers have suggested that additional sampling by region or ecological zone could improve current estimates of biomass. Nevertheless, species-specific relationships may not be needed; even in regions with highly diverse species, measuring the diameter of any type of tree at a height of about four and a half feet provides enough information about the tree's biomass content to explain more than 95 percent of the variation in biomass among different species.[21]

Carbon Content of Biomass. To impute the carbon content of biomass, researchers typically rely on broadly accepted values of about 50 percent. However, the carbon content of forest biomass can vary from 43 percent to 55 percent worldwide and from 43 percent to 49 percent in the tropics.[22]

Improving the Reliability of Measurements of Forest Carbon. Minimizing the uncertainty around each of the four factors used to estimate the amount of carbon stored in forests would be costly. Improving the precision of any one of the factors by a certain proportion would, however, have an equivalent impact on the precision of the final estimate, because the factors are combined multiplicatively to estimate the amount of forest carbon.[23] For example, correcting a 10 percent error in the carbon content of biomass would have the same impact as correcting a 10 percent error in forest area. Thus, information about the relative cost of equivalent percentage increases in the precision of different factors would help identify cost-effective improvements in measuring the amount of forest carbon. The need for such improvements could be assessed in light of the standards for accuracy set by any policies to reduce greenhouse gas emissions that might be put in place in the future. According to existing standards for the estimates of forest carbon that are included in voluntary reporting protocols and scientific inventories, those estimates should have no more than a 5 percent chance of overstating carbon storage.[24]

Improving the Capability of Developing Countries to Measure Changes in Forest Carbon. Even with techniques that could improve estimates of changes in forest carbon, developing countries may not have sufficient technical capabilities to make such estimates. However, those measurements would be needed to determine the compensation to be paid for preserving forestland. Those countries are unlikely to want outsiders in charge of assessing what they have accomplished with their sovereign resources for the purpose of determining the compensation due. Such concerns point to the importance of individual countries having the necessary personnel and technical capabilities to measure changes in their forest carbon rather than having to rely on outside groups to make those measurements.

For 13 of the developing countries that ranked in the top 25 nations for forest-based emissions from 1990 to 2005, some evidence is available about their ability to conduct forest inventories, their experience in acquiring and processing remote-sensing data, and their use of detailed

---

20. Ibid. Fagan and Defries point out that launches of planned satellite missions can fail or be delayed by budgetary and construction issues. Also, the operating life of satellites in orbit can be shorter than expected.

21. Sandra Brown, "Measuring Carbon in Forests: Current Status and Future Challenges," *Environmental Pollution*, vol. 116, no. 3 (March 2002), pp. 363–372.

22. Intergovernmental Panel on Climate Change, *2006 IPCC Guidelines for National Greenhouse Gas Inventories* (prepared by the National Greenhouse Gas Inventories Programme, edited by H.S. Eggleston and others, Hayama, Japan, 2006), Table 4.3, **Error! Hyperlink reference not valid.**|; Fagan and DeFries, *Measurement and Monitoring of the World's Forests*; and Sandra Brown, "Measuring, Monitoring, and Verification of Carbon Benefits for Forest-Based Projects," *Philosophical Transactions of the Royal Society of London*, vol. 360 (2002), pp. 1669–1683.

23. Paul E. Waggoner, *Forest Inventories: Discrepancies and Uncertainties*, RFF Discussion Paper 09-29 (Washington, D.C.: Resources for the Future, August 2009).

24. Molly Macauley and others, *Forest Measurement and Monitoring: Technical Capacity and "How Good is Good Enough?"*

measurements in reporting carbon stock (see Figure 5).[25] That evidence indicates that further capacity-building might improve countries' ability to produce useful measures of changes in forest carbon. Brazil, for example, might develop in-country expertise to conduct forest inventories that would complement the multiple inventories conducted by international consultants or donors. Nonetheless, Brazil is the only one of the 13 countries that has used advanced remote-sensing to monitor changes in forests and is one of only two that have performed their own evaluations of biomass and carbon content by forest type for purposes of carbon reporting (Mexico is the other one). Indonesia has produced only one forest inventory but has done so relying on in-country expertise. Although Indonesia has mapped forest area using standard remote-sensing technologies, unlike Brazil it has yet to use advanced remote-sensing to monitor changes in forests and has based its carbon reporting only on standard values for biomass and carbon content assigned by broad forest type. Five of the 13 countries have no forest inventories and no experience in acquiring and processing remote-sensing data or in reporting forest carbon. [26]

Structuring Incentives to Reduce Forest-Based Emissions

Designing incentives to reduce worldwide forest-based emissions is particularly challenging because such incentives generate direct and indirect effects, often in opposite directions. The direct effect is the reduced rate of deforestation that is the initial response to the incentives. The indirect effects, commonly referred to as "leakage," consist of responses in world markets to the direct effect and tend to offset the direct effect. For example, if incentives succeeded in reducing forest loss in countries receiving

them, the resulting reduction in the supply of agricultural and timber products would probably lead to increases in their prices. Internationally, land values associated with those products would probably rise as a result. If that occurred, deforestation would probably increase in countries that were not receiving incentives, thereby reducing the cost-effectiveness of those incentives.

An effective incentive program requires projections of the amount of deforestation that would occur in the absence of the program and procedures that account for and minimize leakage. Various approaches to providing compensation have different implications both for the magnitude of leakage and for the extent to which programs end up paying for preservation in areas in which forests may not have been at risk of destruction. Thus, they can have an important influence on the cost-effectiveness of forest-based mitigation relative to other ways of reducing GHG emissions.

Baselines for Measuring Reductions. In general, policies that would provide compensation for forest preservation require national baselines from which to measure the reductions in GHG emissions associated with the policies. Consider, for example, a policy in which all developing countries would receive compensation for reducing their rates of deforestation. Under that policy, each country would have a baseline that reflects its historical rate of deforestation, which would be determined by the net rate observed over several past years because rates of deforestation vary significantly from year to year. Each country's baseline would be used to indicate what its behavior would have been in the absence of the policy, including the net effects of activities that preserve forests and those that destroy them.

Such a policy could have substantial direct effects in countries with high baseline rates of deforestation (such as Brazil and Indonesia), and those countries might reduce their rates of deforestation in response to the incentives offered under the policy. However, countries with low baseline rates (such as Gabon and Vietnam) would be likely places for leakage to occur because they would have little room for improvement and because world markets might offer them greater economic benefits from increasing deforestation than they would receive from reducing it.

25. Pat Hardcastle and David Baird, *Capability and Cost Assessment of the Major Forest Nations to Measure and Monitor Their Forest Carbon* (Edinburgh: LTS International, April 7, 2008), www.ibcperu.org/doc/isis/11466.pdf. The 13 countries are Bolivia, Brazil, Cambodia, Cameroon, China, the Democratic Republic of the Congo, Indonesia, Malaysia, Mexico, Myanmar, Papua New Guinea, Peru, and Venezuela.

26. Canada, a developed country with vast forestland, provides a point of reference for the capability of developing countries to carry out those activities. Canada conducts multiple inventories on its own, uses advanced remote sensing, and, in reporting information on biomass and carbon content, differentiates by forest type and evaluates the same sample forest plots over time.

Figure 5.

Capability of Developing Countries to Measure Changes in Forest Carbon

(Number of countries)

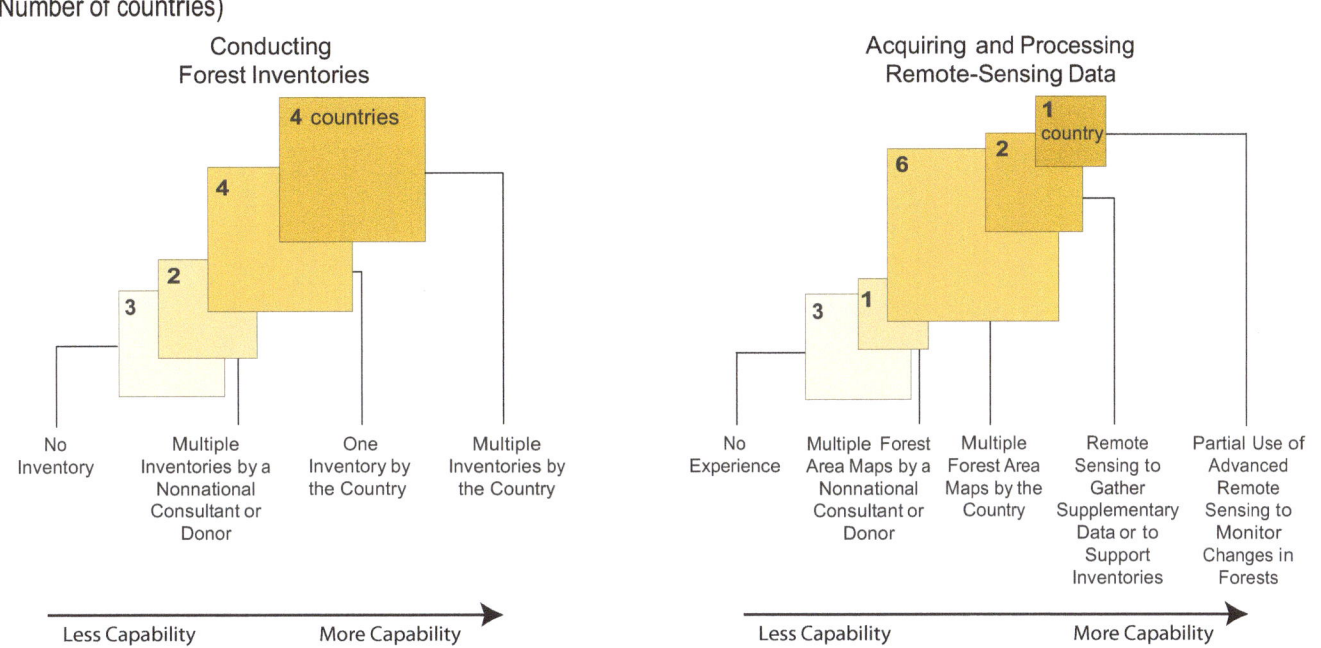

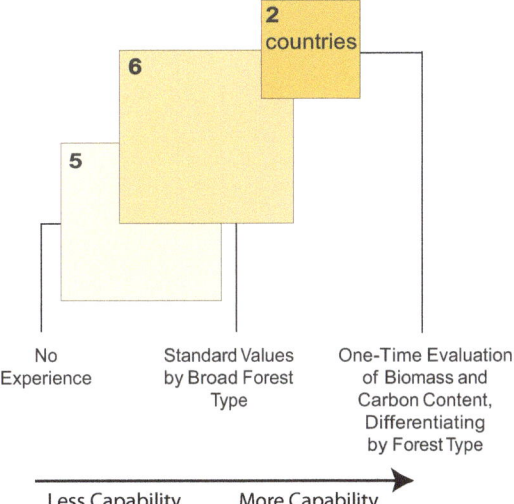

Source: Congressional Budget Office based on data from Pat Hardcastle and David Baird, Capability and Cost Assessment of the Major Forest Nations to Measure and Monitor Their Forest Carbon (Edinburgh: LTS International, April 7, 2008), **Error! Hyperlink reference not valid. Error! Hyperlink reference not valid.**.

Notes: Information on collecting data and measuring and reporting forest carbon is available for 13 of the 25 countries that made the largest contribution to forest-based emissions from 1990 to 2005 (see Figure 3). Those 13 countries are Bolivia, Brazil, Cambodia, Cameroon, China, the Democratic Republic of the Congo, Indonesia, Malaysia, Mexico, Myanmar, Papua New Guinea, Peru, and Venezuela.

Canada, a developed country with vast forestland, provides a point of reference for the capability of developing countries to carry out those activities. Canada conducts multiple inventories on its own, uses advanced remote sensing, and, in reporting information on biomass and carbon content, differentiates by forest type and evaluates the same sample forest plots over time.

a. Obtaining the most useful information on biomass and carbon content requires differentiating by forest type and evaluating the same sample forest over time, but none of the 13 countries had that capability.

Factors That Affect Leakage. In assessing incentives to reduce total forest-based emissions, it is important to consider several factors that influence leakage. First, less leakage would occur if countries representing a greater share of the world's forests participated in the compensation system.

Second, leakage would be smaller if more of the factors that led to deforestation in a country were local. For example, if a program led to the preservation of forests that would otherwise have been cleared to produce agricultural commodities for local markets, then the prices of goods in other countries would not increase. Without price increases, there would be no mechanism to prompt leakage.

Third, the willingness of people to change their patterns of consumption could also suppress leakage. If, for example, forest preservation caused supplies of certain locally produced goods to decline, people might purchase other goods instead—the production of which did not involve deforestation. The reduction in supply attributable to forest preservation would be accompanied by a reduction in demand, and prices would not change. Thus there would be no incentive to destroy forests elsewhere to replace the goods that had been locally produced before the forest preservation program began.

Finally, if production shifted to a location having a lower rate of greenhouse gas emissions, less leakage would occur. The CO_2e content per unit of output might be smaller in a new location if, for example, agricultural productivity per acre of land was higher there.

Assessing the Impact of Leakage. Leakage reduces the cost-effectiveness of programs aiming to achieve global net reductions in forest-based emissions.[27] When leakage occurs, global reductions in greenhouse gases fall short of the policy's intended reductions. In essence, then, leakage means that the actual cost of achieving a given reduction in global greenhouse gases is higher than it appears to be when measured within the limited geographic scope of the policy.

Anticipating the impact of leakage is difficult, however, because it cannot be easily measured. Measuring leakage requires identifying how reduced deforestation in one country affected markets for different products in all other locations. Researchers estimate leakage using economic data and modeling. To date, analyses of leakage from forest preservation have yielded estimates of emissions displaced to other locations that range from single-digit percentages to over 90 percent.[28]

Refining empirical estimates of leakage in the context of specific policies would improve the accuracy of assessments of the policies' costs. Estimates of the cost-effectiveness of forest-based mitigation, for example, are based on the assessment that achieving an additional reduction in GHG emissions through forest preservation is cheaper than doing so through an alternative strategy. For that assessment to hold, the direct cost advantage of reducing emissions through forest-based mitigation cannot be eliminated by leakage. Suppose, for example, that such a reduction suffered 50 percent leakage and that the reduction through the alternative strategy suffered none. For the forest-based mitigation to be worthwhile, its direct cost would have to be no more than half that of the alternative strategy. The greater the leakage differential, the greater the direct cost advantage needed to make forest-based mitigation cost-effective.

Structuring Incentives to Minimize Leakage. Funders of preservation programs might expand participation and minimize leakage by compensating developing countries that had been preserving forests over some period before the policy was in effect. For example, a country whose emissions from deforestation were less than half the global average could be compensated for maintaining that low rate. Alternatively, if those emissions were greater than or equal to the global average, a policy could compensate that country for lowering them. Because the factors affecting leakage vary across countries, however, policies that did not tailor incentives to the circumstances in each particular country might still have substantial leakage even if all countries had some incentives to reduce deforestation under the policy.

27. Leakage is not specific to forest-based mitigation. It can occur with any policy for reducing greenhouse gas emissions that fails to address all potential emitters.

28. Brian C. Murray, "Leakage from an Avoided Deforestation Compensation Policy: Concepts, Empirical Evidence, and Corrective Policy Options," in Charles Palmer and Stephanie Engel, eds., *Avoided Deforestation: Prospects for Mitigating Climate Change* (Oxford, United Kingdom: Routledge, 2009), pp. 151–172.

Figure 6.

Government Effectiveness in Countries Responsible for 95 Percent of Global Forest-Based Emissions, 1990 to 2005

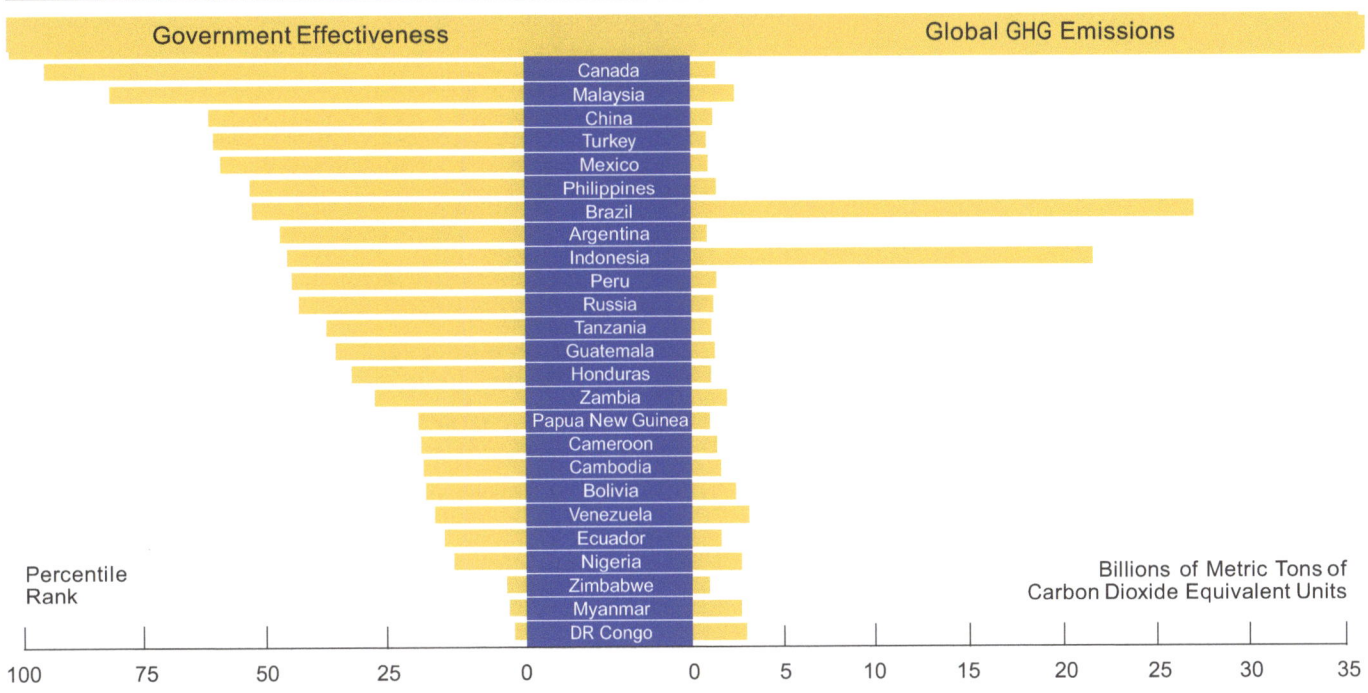

Sources: Congressional Budget Office based on data from World Bank,"Worldwide Governance Indicators" (2010), http://info
.worldbank.org/governance/wgi/sc_country.asp; and World Resources Institute, "Climate Analysis Indicators Tool (CAIT)" (2011),
http://cait.wri.org.

Notes: "Government effectiveness" is a governance indicator reported by the World Bank. It measures the quality of public services, the
quality of the civil service and the degree of its independence from political pressures, the quality of policy formulation and
implementation, and the credibility of the government's commitments to such policies.

GHG = greenhouse gas; DR Congo = Democratic Republic of the Congo.

Instead of basing incentives on differences in forest-based emissions relative to historical rates, a more complicated incentive formula could be used, incorporating projections about future pressures on forests arising from the policy itself, as well as from other economic, social, and institutional factors. Finding adequate data on the relevant economic, social, and institutional variables could be difficult, as could reaching agreement on which values for those variables—from among a range of defensible ones—to use in the projections.

Improving Governance in Developing Countries
The quality of a nation's governance influences its ability to implement policies and to deal with forces that undermine that ability, such as political instability and corruption. With inadequate governance, even programs that offer payment for reducing deforestation might not result in more preservation.

Governments' Effectiveness. One indicator of governance is government effectiveness. That indicator reflects a country's capacity for establishing reliable programs, such as those to reduce forest-based GHG emissions. According to the World Bank, which tracks and reports measures of governance, government effectiveness can be measured by the quality of public services, the quality of the civil service and the degree of its independence from political pressures, the quality of policy formulation and implementation, and the credibility of the government's commitments to such policies.[29]

Countries with an ineffective government might have difficulty producing verifiable reductions in emissions, even when programs for forest preservation are in place. Of the

29. World Bank, "Worldwide Governance Indicators" (2009),
http://info.worldbank.org/governance/wgi/pdf/ge.pdf.

25 countries with the largest forest-based emissions from 1990 to 2005, nearly three-quarters rank in the bottom half of all countries on measures of effective government (see Figure 6); they accounted for 55 percent of the world's forest-based GHG emissions. The two largest emitters, Brazil and Indonesia, are at roughly the 50th percentile for government effectiveness. By comparison, the government effectiveness rating for Canada, which is also in the top 25 producers of forest-based GHG emissions, is well above the 90th percentile.

In a weak government, the agencies responsible for preserving forests may have conflicting goals or inadequate authority for managing land use. For example, some countries may designate a forested area for both conservation and production—two competing uses of land.

Government agencies also may lack effective mechanisms for determining the amount of compensation and distributing it to indigenous peoples, local communities, and individuals who own forests, thereby undermining preservation efforts (see Box 2). In Brazil, for example, the process for determining compensation would be greatly improved if the appropriate agencies were able to map coordinates from satellite imagery to rural properties for which there is clearly established ownership. As of 2008, however, the government had only just started a pilot project to create that type of mapping and was doing so in only one of the nine Amazonian states.[30] In Cameroon, relatively strong forestry laws have been undermined because the local communities have not received adequate incentives from the national government to preserve forests.[31]

Poor governance may also mean that the rights to control forest resources are not clearly defined, making the gains from immediate use by clearing the land for agricultural production, timber, or wood for fuel more certain than the gains from preserving the forest. In Ghana, for example, landowners do not necessarily hold the right to the timber on their property. The lack of clarity about ownership creates incentives for farmers to log trees on their land to prevent timber companies with legal access to those trees from doing so and, in the process, damaging the farmers' cocoa crops.[32] In Brazil, a long-standing land statute, recently amended to counter abuse, allowed anyone who made "effective use" of the land to take a first step toward owning it, even without prior legal title. Forest clearing in that country, usually considered proof of such use, is a way to gain formal title to land owned by others and a way for landowners to prevent others from laying claim to their land.[33]

In some countries, the traditional claims of local populations that may support forest preservation often give way to statutory claims by others seeking to make greater use of forests' resources. In Indonesia, for example, one nongovernmental organization documented over 500 ongoing land conflicts between local communities and companies involved in producing palm oil.[34]

Corruption and Political Instability. Other aspects of governance, such as corruption and political instability, can also undermine efforts to preserve forests. National plans classifying forests for preservation might be intentionally structured to generate benefits for specific interests, but even if they are not, laws to protect forests can be ineffective if government officials ignore violations so they can personally benefit.

Little research has been done on the general relationship between corruption and forest loss. One study of African nations found no significant connection, and a broader study of countries across the globe found an association between a reduction in perceived corruption and lower

30. Paulo Barreto, "Implications of the Climate Change Debate on Land Tenure in the Brazilian Amazon" (speech for the Conference on New Challenges for Land Policy and Administration, World Bank, Washington, D.C., February 14–15, 2008).

31. Environmental Audit Committee, *Reducing Greenhouse Gas Emissions from Deforestation: No Hope Without Forests* (United Kingdom, House of Commons, June 16 2009), **Error! Hyperlink reference not valid.**Error! Hyperlink reference not valid.. See also Marcelin Tonye Mahop, "Forestry and Environmental Regulations, Legal Protection and Enforcement of Community Rights in Cameroon," *IUP Journal of Governance and Public Policy*, vol. 4, no. 1 (March 2009), pp. 7–21.

32. C.P. Hansen and T. Treue, "Assessing Illegal Logging in Ghana," *International Forestry Review*, vol. 10, no. 4 (2008), pp. 573–590.

33. Kathryn R. Kirby and others, "The Future of Deforestation in the Brazilian Amazon," *Future*, vol. 38 (2006), pp. 432–453.

34. Sawit Watch, "Issues Surrounding Indonesian Palm Oil Industry" (memorandum submitted to the Delegation of the European Commission to Indonesia, July 24, 2009), http://normanjiwan.blogspot.com/2009_07_01_archive.html.

Box 2.

The Role of Local Populations in Forest Preservation

Researchers emphasize the role of indigenous peoples and other forest-dependent communities in the success of efforts to preserve forests. An estimated 7 percent of public land in developing countries is reserved for those groups, who also own an estimated 57 percent of private lands in those countries. Overall, local populations control an estimated total of at least 19 percent of the land in developing countries.[1]

Local populations can contribute to the preservation of forests regardless of whether they have official control over that land. Forestland under national control may be difficult to preserve because of corruption or lack of resources for enforcement; engaging the participation of local communities might be a better way to preserve forests. For example, the Nepalese Forest Act of 1993 redirected the Department of Forests "from protecting national forests towards building forest user groups to manage all of the nation's forestland without interference from outside of the community." One study of the impact of that law found that households' consumption of wood for fuel in areas in which user groups were involved in forest management was about 14 percent lower than in comparable areas without user groups, suggesting that harvests were being restrained to promote regeneration of degraded forests.[2] Other studies

have found that territories officially recognized as belonging to indigenous peoples have been effective in reducing deforestation in the Brazilian Amazon.[3]

Conversely, preservation efforts may be undermined by populations that depend on forests for their livelihood. In the absence of incentives for preservation, community-controlled forestland might be converted to agriculture or managed for forest products in a way that increased greenhouse gas emissions. Forest preservation programs that fail to compensate local populations for new limits on their access to the resources they have traditionally relied on, or that fail to equitably distribute compensation for preservation, could jeopardize the support of local communities. Local populations could oppose new forest preservation projects, and social unrest could undermine political support for such projects. For example, the Tropical Forestry Action Plan, an international forest preservation initiative in the late 1980s and early 1990s, lost political support in part because the plan was designed without sufficient participation of indigenous peoples and other forest-dependent communities. It neglected differences between national concerns for forest preservation and such local concerns as community claims to forest resources, community benefits from logging, and assistance with economic development.[4] Recent international accords, such as the Cancun Agreement of the United Nations Framework Convention on Climate Change, assert the importance of involving forest-dependent communities in making decisions and managing forest preservation in a socially responsible way.

---

1. There is much more public land than private land in those countries. The Congressional Budget Office made these estimates using government data on land ownership in 18 developing countries that are among the world's 30 most heavily forested countries. The data underlying the estimates are from William D. Sunderlin, Jeffrey Hatcher, and Megan Lidle, *From Exclusion to Ownership? Challenges and Opportunities in Advancing Forest Tenure Reform* (Washington, D.C.: Rights and Resources Group, 2008), p. 8, Table 1, www.rightsandresources.org/documents/files/doc_736.pdf. The government data do not reflect the amount of forested land actively claimed by indigenous or other local communities.

2. Eric V. Edmonds, "Government Initiated Community Resource Management and Local Resource Extraction from Nepal's Forests," *Journal of Development Economics*, vol. 68, no. 1 (June 2002), pp. 89–115.

3. D. Nepstad and others, "Inhibition of Amazon Deforestation and Fire by Parks and Indigenous Lands," *Conservation Biology*, vol. 20, no. 1 (2006), pp. 65–73; and Britaldo Soares-Filho and others, "Role of Brazilian Amazon Protected Areas in Climate Change Mitigation," *Proceedings of the National Academy of Sciences*, vol. 107, no. 24 (2010), pp. 10821–10826.

4. Alexander Pfaff and others, *Policy Impacts on Deforestation: Lessons Learned from Past Experiences to Inform New Initiatives* (Durham, N.C.: Duke University, Nicholas Institute for Environmental Policy Solutions, June 2010).

rates of deforestation.[35] Some studies document how bribery undermines policies that protect forests, and anecdotal reports of corruption include cases in which timber has been harvested without a legal permit.[36] A recent report on forest reform in Liberia concluded that all existing logging contracts had been granted in violation of national laws; the report also noted widespread irregularities in the bidding process.[37] In the Democratic Republic of the Congo, some segments of the army, in addition to militia groups, profited from trade in illegally produced charcoal made from the forest resources of a national park.[38]

Political instability also can undermine efforts to improve forest governance. Following an unconstitutional change in Madagascar's government in March 2009, for example, the United States and other countries suspended all aid to that country except humanitarian or emergency aid. Observers have noted recent reversals of the forest preservation in that country that had resulted from nearly two decades of involvement by donor countries in developing management systems for protected areas, promoting alternatives to slash-and-burn agriculture, and improving environmental practices.[39]

Efforts to Improve Governance. Countries that donate or lend money to developing countries have taken various approaches to improve the governance of forests. Those approaches include promoting sustainable forestry practices and standards for timber products, making the receipt of international lending contingent on reforms, funding the formulation of national action plans, and reducing the international debt of countries that establish conservation trust funds. But there are no quantitative evaluations of efforts to improve forest governance, and anecdotal evidence is mixed.

Programs to improve governance may fail because of insufficient funding or inadequate design.[40] In designing programs, for example, policymakers may not pay enough attention to the potential for leakage, which can undermine a program's goals. The European Union (EU) has been negotiating bilateral agreements with tropical countries. In cases in which negotiations have been completed, the EU has committed funding to strengthen enforcement of laws governing forests.[41] Then, following an agreed-upon period of investment, the EU will import designated wood products from those countries only if a certificate confirms the legality of their supply chain. However, some evidence indicates that timber from participating countries may be delivered to the EU through other countries, circumventing the aim of the agreements.

Policy Approaches for Reducing Forest-Based Emissions

Approaches that the United States and other developed countries might pursue to support forest-based mitigation in developing countries fall into two broad categories:

■ Providing financial and technical assistance to governments interested in preserving forests and

35. Smith and others, "Governance and the Loss of Biodiversity," *Nature*, vol. 426, no. 6962 (November 6, 2003), pp. 67–70; and Edward B. Barbier, Richard Damania, and Daniel Léonard, "Corruption, Trade and Resource Conversion," *Journal of Environmental Economics and Management*, vol. 50, no. 2 (September 2005), pp. 276–299.

36. Smith and others, "Governance and the Loss of Biodiversity"; Anne Casson and Krystof Obidzinski, "From New Order to Regional Autonomy: Shifting Dynamics of Illegal Logging in Kalimantan, Indonesia," in Luca Tacconi, ed., *Illegal Logging: Law Enforcement, Livelihoods and the Timber Trade* (London: Earthscan, 2007); and Douglas Dewitt Southgate Jr. and others, "Markets, Institutions, and Forestry: The Consequences of Timber Trade Liberalization in Ecuador," *World Development*, vol. 28, no. 11 (November 2000), pp. 2005–2012.

37. Sustainable Development Institute, *Liberia—The Promise Betrayed* (January 2010), www.sdiliberia.org/sites/default/files/documents/ Promise%20Betrayed.pdf.

38. United Press International, "Charcoal Trade Funds Congo Conflict," UPI.com (July 31, 2009), www.upi.com/ Top_News/2009/07/31/Charcoal-trade-funds-Congo-conflict/ UPI-81621249086595.

39. Andrew C. Revkin, "Madagascar Forest Defenders Send S.O.S.," *New York Times*, March 20, 2009; and Linda Pressly, "Madagascar's Forests Plundered for Rare Rosewood," *BBC Radio 4, Crossing Continents* (August 5, 2010), www.bbc.co.uk/news/world-africa-10765418.

40. For a review of design issues for efforts to conserve forests, see Alexander Pfaff and others, *Policy Impacts on Deforestation: Lessons Learned from Past Experiences to Inform New Initiatives* (Durham, N.C.: Duke University, Nicholas Institute for Environmental Policy Solutions, June 2010).

41. To date, the EU has agreements with Cameroon, the Central African Republic, Ghana, Indonesia, Liberia, Malaysia, and the Republic of the Congo.

■ Creating demand in private markets for reductions in forest-based greenhouse gas emissions.

Providing financial and technical assistance would focus directly on addressing the challenges to reducing forest-based emissions. Creating demand in private markets could mobilize substantial funding for that effort. Although the two strategies can be pursued independently, they might work better in tandem. The viability of markets, for example, might depend on having in place a reliable program for achieving measurable reductions in forest-based emissions—the type of program that financial and technical assistance can help establish.

Assistance to Governments

Financial and technical assistance from developed countries could help address the more tractable challenges—measuring changes in forest-based greenhouse gases and creating incentives for cost-effective global net reductions in forest-based emissions. Whether such assistance could improve forest governance in developing countries is less clear.

Although the precise amount of assistance currently provided for forest-related activities is unknown, estimates to date suggest that providing sufficient funding to substantially reduce deforestation in developing countries could be difficult. All types of such assistance averaged roughly $560 million annually from the mid-1990s through 2008, or about $2.8 billion over a five-year period.[42] Another rough estimate puts the cost of setting up the capacity and infrastructure needed to operate a reliable program for reducing deforestation in a developing country that has the political will to carry out such a program at about $95 million over five years.[43] Together, the two estimates suggest that if historical amounts of aid were

fully dedicated to preparing willing countries to run reliable programs for reducing deforestation, they might ready as many as 30 such countries to operate such programs.

Additional funds would be needed, however, to compensate those who reduce forest-based GHG emissions, and developed countries recognize that need. Six nations—Australia, France, Japan, Norway, the United Kingdom, and the United States—recently pledged to provide $3.5 billion over three years to encourage forest preservation in developing countries. The pledge was in keeping with a collective commitment made by developed countries to provide an initial $30 billion in resources over the 2010–2012 period to facilitate the adaptation to and mitigation of climate change. Although the commitments are explicit, whether they are in addition to existing ones is unclear, and whether the funds will be delivered is uncertain because some funds are contingent on the approval of the budgets of donor countries.[44] Fulfilling those commitments could ultimately depend on the extent to which forest preservation reduces the cost of meeting any goals that developed countries adopt for reducing emissions and on the competing demands in those countries for government funds.

With the challenges of improving governance and the potential limitations on funding, an effective strategy might be to direct assistance toward selected countries that have relatively strong governance and are rich in threatened forest resources. Of the 25 countries primarily responsible for global forest-based emissions in recent decades, Brazil, Indonesia, Venezuela, the Democratic Republic of the Congo, and Myanmar were the top five emitters, accounting for 69 percent of total forest-based emissions. Of the five, Brazil and Indonesia have comparatively strong governance (see Figure 6 on page 15). They also have remaining forest resources that account for roughly 40 percent of the total forest area in tropical

42. Search of "Query Wizard for International Development Statistics" (Organisation for Economic Co-operation and Development, Paris), http://stats.oecd.org/qwids.

43. That very rough estimate is based on the costs of past efforts to reform policies and institutions in developing countries. Whether the costs of previous interventions are a good indicator of the amounts needed for reform is not certain. In addition, the projects have not always achieved the desired outcomes. See Eliasch Review, *Climate Change: Financing Global Forests* (prepared by Johan Eliasch, 2008), p. 219, www.official-documents.gov.uk/ document/other/9780108507632/9780108507632.pdf; and personal communication to the Congressional Budget Office by a staff member of Chatham House, Royal Institute of International Affairs, United Kingdom, November 20, 2010.

44. A recent agreement at the Cancun conference of the United Nations Framework Convention on Climate Change (UNFCCC) invited developed countries to submit an annual document presenting information on the resources they have provided to fulfill the commitment and on how developing countries obtain the resources. See UNFCCC, "Addendum, Part Two: Action Taken by the Conference of the Parties at Its Sixteenth Session," Decision 1/CP.16 (December 2010), p. 16, http://unfccc.int/resource/ docs/2010/cop16/eng/07a01.pdf#page=2.

developing nations.[45] Establishing and supporting successful forest-based mitigation programs in those two countries could help preserve a significant proportion of tropical forests worldwide and might serve as a foundation for a similar effort encompassing other tropical developing nations. Such a broader effort would be important if leakage associated with the more focused program was significant. Because roughly 60 percent of the total forest area in developing tropical countries lies outside Brazil and Indonesia, significant leakage could occur, which would undermine the potential climate benefits of preserving the forests in those two countries.[46]

Markets for Reductions in Forest-Based GHG Emissions

Funding for forest preservation in developing countries might also be available in private markets. To date, markets for forest carbon have been largely voluntary rather than prompted by regulation. They exist primarily because of individuals' and businesses' perceptions of social responsibility and efforts to comply with expected climate policies even before the policies have been announced. Historically, those factors have motivated over three-quarters of the transactions in the market for forest carbon. Markets directed only about $10.4 million in funding to forest preservation in 2009, avoiding 3.6 million tons of CO_2e emissions at an average price of $2.90 per ton. They generated more funding for planting forests (about $23.6 million at $4.70 per ton) and for managing forests (about $11.2 million at $7.40 per ton)—activities that have less biological potential to reduce emissions than does preservation.[47] In 2010, encouraged by the attention paid to forest preservation in

international policy discussions, market funding for preservation climbed to $87.4 million, avoiding 19.4 million tons of CO_2e emissions at an average price of $4.50 a ton. Funding for planting new forests declined slightly, to $22.1 million, and funding for managing forests increased slightly, to $13.4 million.[48]

To date, regulations have motivated only about one-quarter of the transactions in the markets for forest carbon. To increase market funding for preservation, forest-based reductions in GHG emissions could be sold in markets fostered by cap-and-trade programs or by tax credits that might accompany taxes on GHG emissions.[49] Such markets might motivate substantial increases in funding if forest-based mitigation abroad offered the opportunity to comply with required reductions in greenhouse gas emissions at a lower cost than that for reducing domestic emissions under a cap-and-trade program, for example. The more stringent the limit on emissions in a cap-and-trade program, the greater the potential for generating funding for forest preservation. Similarly, forest-based mitigation abroad might generate tax credits that could offset the impact of a carbon tax imposed on domestic GHG emissions, and the potential for generating funding for forest preservation would reflect the size of the tax.

Under either type of program, the potential funding for forest preservation would depend on the program's rules related to forest-based mitigation abroad. A cap-and-trade program, for example, might allow all or part of participants' GHG emission reductions to come from forest-based activities in foreign countries. It could also specify which countries were eligible for generating forest-based compliance. Similarly, a tax credit for forest preservation could fully or partially offset a domestic entity's related GHG tax liability, and the government

45. Hardcastle and Baird, *Capability and Cost Assessment of the Major Forest Nations to Measure and Monitor Their Forest Carbon,* www.ibcperu.org/doc/isis/11466.pdf.

46. Brazil and Indonesia have slowed their deforestation rates in recent years. Estimated annual deforestation in Brazil declined from 2.9 million hectares during the 1990s to 2.6 million hectares during the subsequent decade. In Indonesia, it declined from 1.9 million hectares to 560,000 hectares. See Food and Agriculture Organization of the United Nations, *Global Forest Resources Assessment,* FAO Forestry Paper 163 (Rome: FAO, 2010), p. 21, www.fao.org/docrep/013/i1757e/i1757e00.htm.

47. Katherine Hamilton and others, *Building Bridges: State of the Voluntary Carbon Markets 2010* (report by Ecosystem Marketplace, Washington, D.C., and Bloomberg New Energy Finance, New York, June 2010), http://moderncms.ecosystemmarketplace .com/repository/moderncms_documents/vcarbon_2010.2.pdf.

48. David Diaz, Katherine Hamilton, and Evan Johnson, *State of the Forest Carbon Markets: From Canopy to Currency* (report by Ecosystem Marketplace, Washington D.C., September 2011), www.forest-trends.org/documents/files/doc_2963.pdf.

49. In the United States, such provisions appeared in bills considered by the 111th Congress. State and regional programs in the United States may provide funding for reducing deforestation in developing countries. Under the Global Warming Solutions Act, for example, California is actively considering such provisions. See Diaz, Hamilton, and Johnson, *State of the Forest Carbon Markets 2011,* www.forest-trends.org/documents/files/doc_2963.pdf.

could specify the countries in which forest-based activities would be eligible for generating credits.

The few existing regulatory programs do not credit emission reductions to forest preservation activities. However, some programs allow participants to meet a portion of their obligation by planting new forests. They include the Regional Greenhouse Gas Initiative (which requires power plants relying on fossil fuels in member states in the northeastern United States to reduce emissions) and the emissions trading systems of the European Union and New Zealand (which facilitate compliance with commitments to reduce emissions under the Kyoto Protocol of the United Nations Framework Convention on Climate Change).[50]

Even if markets established as a result of regulations provide greater financing for forest preservation, they are not necessarily well suited to support reliable programs for reducing forest-based greenhouse gas emissions. Meeting the three challenges—measuring changes in the amount of carbon stored in forests, creating incentives for cost-effective global reductions in forest-based emissions, and improving governance—generally requires up-front financing that is not directly linked to the purchase of the reductions in greenhouse gases accomplished through forest preservation. However, if regulatory programs specified the conditions under which they would credit emission reductions to forest preservation activities, the potential cost savings from use of those credits could motivate firms (or groups of firms in industries with high greenhouse gas emissions) to make investments to address the three challenges. In particular, funding generated by a market-based program for reducing greenhouse gas emissions could help pay for improving measurement of forest carbon in developing countries or for preserving forests in countries where leakage might occur. The potential effect of such funding on governance in developing countries is less clear; it would depend, in part, on how governments would weigh the gains associated with qualifying for market participation against the costs they would incur in designing and implementing policies to preserve forests. For example, concerns that the distribution of associated benefits might create political tensions could make governments reluctant to increase forest preservation.

---

50. Under New Zealand's Emission Trading System, owners of older forests have to submit emission allowances for deforestation, but they are initially granted adequate allowances for that purpose. Owners may choose to sell those allowances if they do not plan to clear forests or if they anticipate that they can profit by selling the allowances and then—at a future time, when they clear forested land—by purchasing replacements at a lower cost.